Overview *Ice-Skating*

A girl skating at an ice rink tells about ice-skating indoors and outdoors.

Reading Vocabulary Words
smooth
safe
rink

High-Frequency Words
ice   cold
good   fun
like   snow
big   outside

Building Future Vocabulary
These vocabulary words do not appear in this text. They are provided to develop related oral vocabulary that first appears in future texts.

Words:	*blur*	*hear*	*trick*
Levels:	Gold	Green	Green

Comprehension Strategy
Comparing and contrasting information

Fluency Skill
Matching character's tone

Phonics Skill
Reading simple one-syllable words and high-frequency words

Reading-Writing Connection
Writing a journal entry

Home Connection
Send home one of the Flying Colors Take-Home books for children to share with their families.

Differentiated Instruction
Before reading the text, query children to discover their level of understanding of the comprehension strategy — Comparing and contrasting information. As you work together, provide additional support to children who show a beginning mastery of the strategy.

Focus on ELL
- If possible, bring in a pair of ice skates for children to inspect. Together point to and name the parts of a skate.

- Help children understand that an indoor ice rink has ice all year long. Have children pantomime ice-skating.

T1

Using This Teaching Version

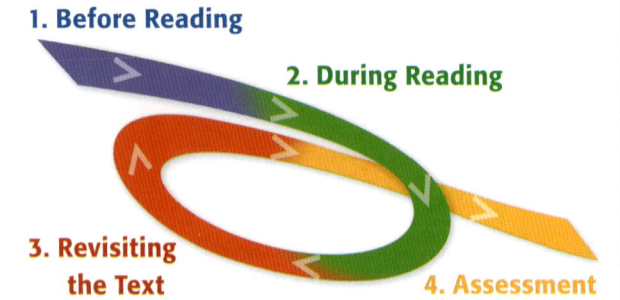

1. Before Reading

2. During Reading

3. Revisiting the Text

4. Assessment

This Teaching Version will assist you in directing children through the process of reading.

1. **Begin with Before Reading** to familiarize children with the book's content. Select the skills and strategies that meet the needs of your children.

2. **Next, go to During Reading** to help children become familiar with the text, and then to read individually on their own.

3. **Then, go back to Revisiting the Text** and select those specific activities that meet children's needs.

4. **Finally, finish with Assessment** to confirm children are ready to move forward to the next text.

1 Before Reading

Building Background

- Write *rink* on the board. Read it aloud. Have children share what they know about skating rinks. (They are indoor or outdoor places with large, flat areas of ice where you can skate or play ice hockey.) Correct any misinformation.

- Introduce the book by reading the title, talking about the cover illustration and photograph, and sharing the overview.

Building Future Vocabulary

Use Interactive Modeling Card: Word Wheel

- Introduce the word *blur*. Ask *What does it mean when some people in a picture are just a blur?* (You can't see them very well.)

- Write the word *blur* in the center of the Word Wheel. Ask children to brainstorm words to complete the wheel.

Introduction to Reading Vocabulary

- On blank cards write: *smooth*, *safe*, and *rink*. Read them aloud. Tell children these words will appear in the text of *Ice-Skating*.

- Use each word in a sentence for understanding.

Introduction to Comprehension Strategy

- Explain that a good way to understand and remember what you read is to compare and contrast, or look for similarities and differences.
- Tell children they will be comparing and contrasting indoor and outdoor ice-skating in *Ice-Skating*.
- Using the cover illustration and photograph, have children tell differences they see between the groups of children.

Introduction to Phonics

- List the following words on the board: **ice**, **good**, **like**, **big**, **cold**, **fun**, **snow**, **outside**.
- Point out that most of these words have only one syllable. Ask *Which word has two syllables?* Tell children that the word **outside** is made of two smaller words. Have children name the two smaller words in **outside**.
- Write the words on index cards and hold them up, one at a time. Ask children to say the word on the card. Continue increasing the speed until children can read each word upon seeing it.

Modeling Fluency

- Read aloud page 2 in a moderate, storytelling tone. Tell children that the narrator is telling a story, much as you would tell a story to a friend.
- Talk about matching your reading tone of voice to the character in the book to help the listener hear and understand the story better.

2 During Reading

Book Talk

Beginning on page T4, use the During Reading notes on the left-hand side to engage children in a book talk. On page 16, follow with Individual Reading.

During Reading

Book Talk

- **Comprehension Strategy** Ask *How are the title page and cover of the book different?* (The cover has photographs and illustrations; the title page just has illustrations. The cover has real people on it; the title page does not.)

- Discuss the title page illustration. Explain that these people are at an ice rink. Encourage children to make predictions about who these people are.

- Introduce the Nonfiction Questions and Answers Interactive Modeling Card. Return to the card as needed to record what children know along with their questions and answers.

Turn to page 2 — Book Talk

T4

Revisiting the Text

Future Vocabulary

- Look at the photograph on the cover. Ask *What kind of trick are the girls in the photograph doing?* (holding on to each other as they skate)

- Ask *What kind of trick is the girl on the title page doing?* (jumping off the ice)

Now revisit pages 2–3

1

During Reading

Book Talk

- **Comprehension Strategy** Ask *What is the difference between the pictures on these pages?* (One is a photograph, one is an illustration; the photograph shows people ice-skating; the illustration shows people getting ready to go ice-skating.) Ask *What are the similarities?* (Both are about people ice-skating.)

- Ask *Do you see the red and blue lines on the ice in the rink? What do you think those are for?* (games of ice hockey)

Turn to page 4 — Book Talk

I like ice-skating.
My brother Marco likes ice-skating, too.
We go to an ice-skating rink.

We put on our ice skates.
Marco has black ice skates.
I have white ice skates.

Revisiting the Text

Future Vocabulary
- Say *Look at the people skating on page 2. Some of them look like a* **blur** *on the ice.* Ask *Why is that?* (They are moving fast. When you take a picture of someone moving, it often comes out **blur**ry.)

Now revisit pages 4–5

During Reading

Book Talk

- **Comprehension Strategy** Ask *How are Marco and the narrator similar?* (They both like to ice-skate.) Ask *How are they different?* (The narrator likes to go slow; Marco likes to go fast. The narrator has white skates; Marco has black ones.)
- **Phonics Skill** Have children locate the words *like, good,* and *ice* on these pages and read them aloud.

Turn to page 6 – Book Talk

I like to go slowly on the ice.
Marco likes to go fast on the ice.
Marco can skate faster than I can.

We see a girl jumping.
We see a boy skating backward.
The girl and boy are good at skating!

Revisiting the Text

Future Vocabulary

- Ask *What tricks are the girl and boy doing on the ice?* (The girl is jumping and the boy is skating backward.)

- Ask *What does it mean to play a trick on someone?* (to fool them or surprise them somehow) *What do we mean when we say that our mind is playing tricks on us?* (It means we are imagining something that might not have happened.)

Now revisit pages 6–7

During Reading

Book Talk

- **Comprehension Strategy** Ask *Does the ice look smooth or rough?* (rough) *Which do you think would be easier to ice-skate on?* (smooth) *Why?* (The blades of your skates wouldn't get caught; you could glide more easily.)

- Explain to children how the machine keeps the ice smooth. Tell children that the machine is known as an ice-resurfacing machine.

➤ *Turn to page 8 – Book Talk*

Ice is made from very cold water.

A big machine keeps the ice smooth at the ice-skating rink.

Revisiting the Text

Future Vocabulary

- Ask children to imagine they can **hear** the machine on page 7 as it smoothes the ice. Ask *Is the machine loud?* (yes)

- Ask *What does it mean when we say we can* **hear** *our own thoughts?* (that we are thinking words as though they are being spoken)

Now revisit pages 8–9

During Reading

Book Talk

- **Comprehension Strategy** Ask *How is this frozen surface different from the indoor rink?* (It only exists when it's cold enough; it's outside.) Ask *How is it similar?* (It's ice; people are skating on it.)
- **Phonics Skill** Have children locate the words *cold, snow, ice, fun,* and *outside.* Have them repeat the words after you.

Turn to page 10 – Book Talk

In some places,
it is very cold in winter.
Snow falls.
Water turns to ice.

Boys and girls have fun outside.
They play in the snow.
They skate on the ice, too.

Revisiting the Text

Future Vocabulary
- **Comprehension Strategy** Ask *What kinds of things would you hear at an outdoor rink?* (the sounds of the skates against the ice, birds, people talking) Ask *What kinds of things would you hear at an indoor rink?* (It would be louder because the skaters are inside a building. You would hear music playing and people laughing and yelling.)

Now revisit pages 10–11

During Reading

Book Talk

- **Comprehension Strategy** Ask *Is an outdoor skating rink as safe as an indoor one? Why or why not?* (If the outdoor rink is on a frozen pond or lake, it may not be frozen enough to skate on.)

- Ask *What is one way to make sure you stay safe on an outdoor ice-skating rink?* (stay with your mom and dad or other adult)

➔ *Turn to page 12 – Book Talk*

In some places,
it is not safe to skate on the ice.

Stay with Mom or Dad.
Skate where it is safe.

Revisiting the Text

Future Vocabulary
- Ask children to imagine they are next to the family on the ice on page 11. Ask *What kinds of things would you hear?* (the girl laughing, the parents encouraging her to keep skating)

- Tell children that courts hold a hearing for people who are charged with crimes. The court hears about the crime and decides what should happen next.

Now revisit pages 12–13

During Reading

Book Talk

- Ask *Which kind of skating rink does the narrator like best?* (indoor) Ask *Why?* (She feels safe there.)
- Ask *What are some things that make you feel safe?* (seatbelts, handrails, bike helmets, sidewalks) *Who are some people who make you feel safe?* (parent, teacher, crossing guard)

Turn to page 14 — Book Talk

Revisiting the Text

Future Vocabulary
- Point out the girl who has fallen on the ice. Ask children to tell about a time when they fell. Do they remember details or is the actual fall just a blur in their minds?

Now revisit pages 14–15

During Reading

Book Talk

- Ask *What does the narrator like about the skating rink?* (She can do things with her friends.)
- Ask children to describe the clothing that the characters are wearing on these pages. Ask *How are these children dressed differently from the people on page 11?* (They aren't wearing outdoor clothing.)

Turn to page 16 – Book Talk

We see our friends at the skating rink.
We hold hands with our friends.
We like to play games, too.

My friends help me up if I fall down.

15

Revisiting the Text

Future Vocabulary
- Ask *Why did the illustrator blur out the rest of the ice-skating rink and just show the characters?* (to focus on the girl and her friends)

Go to page T5 – Revisiting the Text

15

During Reading

Book Talk
- Leave this page for children to discover on their own when they read the book individually.

Individual Reading
Have each child read the entire book at his or her own pace while remaining in the group.

Go to page T5 – Revisiting the Text

During independent work time, children can read the online book at:
www.rigbyflyingcolors.com

Revisiting the Text

Future Vocabulary
- Use the notes on the right-hand pages to develop oral vocabulary that goes beyond the text. These vocabulary words first appear in future texts. These words are: *blur*, *hear*, and *trick*.

Turn back to page 1

Reading Vocabulary Review
Activity Sheet: Word Wheel

- Have children write the word *smooth* in the center of the Word Wheel.
- Together brainstorm other words that mean the same and opposite of *smooth* and write them in the Word Wheel.

Comprehension Strategy Review
Use Interactive Modeling Card: Venn Diagram

- Write *Outdoor Ice-Skating Rink* over the left circle of the Venn Diagram and *Indoor Ice-Skating Rink* over the right circle.
- Together, complete the diagram with characteristics of ice-skating rinks.

Phonics Review
- Have children make lists of simple one-syllable words from the story. *(ice, good, fun)* Have them read their lists aloud to a partner.
- Partners can then exchange lists and write sentences using each word at least once.

Fluency Review
- Ask children to read page 16 to a partner in a tone of voice that reflects the way the narrator probably feels.
- Remind children that matching a character's tone of voice makes a story more interesting to hear and easier to remember.

Reading-Writing Connection
Activity Sheet: Nonfiction Questions and Answers

To assist children with linking reading and writing:
- Have children use the Nonfiction Questions and Answers sheet to identify what they might still want to know about ice-skating rinks.
- Have children use the completed sheet to write a journal entry describing a day of ice-skating.

4 Assessment

Assessing Future Vocabulary

Work with each child individually. Ask questions that elicit each child's understanding of the Future Vocabulary words. Note each child's responses:

- Why might you not remember things clearly if they are a blur in your mind?
- If you hear a train whistle, why should you be careful near railroad crossings?
- What kinds of tricks does a magician do?

Assessing Comprehension Strategy

Work with each child individually. Note each child's understanding of comparing and contrasting information:

- Which ice-skating rink would be the loudest, indoor or outdoor? Why?
- To which ice-skating rink could you wear jeans and a T-shirt? Why?
- Which ice-skating rink is likely to be safer? Why?
- Which ice-skating rink is dependent on the weather? Why?

Assessing Phonics

Work with each child individually. Use the cards of one- and two-syllable words you made earlier. Hold up each card and ask the child to read the word. Note each child's responses for understanding one-syllable and high-frequency words:

- Use the following words: *ice, good, like, big, cold, fun, snow, outside.*
- Did each child recognize one-syllable words?
- Did each child recognize that two-syllable words are sometimes made up of two smaller words?

Assessing Fluency

Have each child read page 5 to you. Note each child's understanding of matching tone of voice to the character's tone of voice:

- Was each child able to correctly assess the character's feelings in order to match the character's tone of voice?
- Was each child able to read simple one-syllable words?
- Did each child pause at commas and take a breath at the ends of sentences?

Interactive Modeling Cards

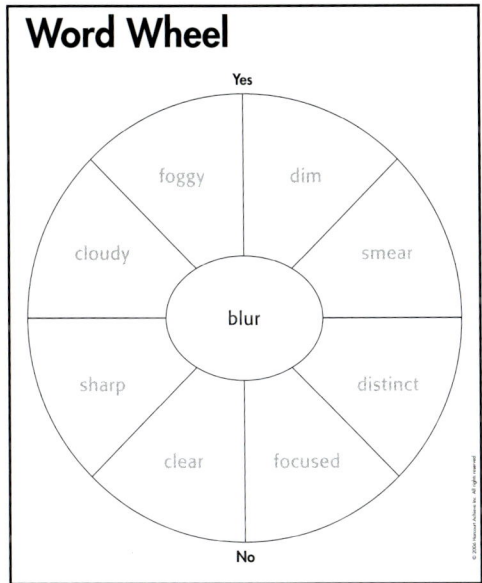

Directions: With children, fill in the Word Wheel using the word *blur*.

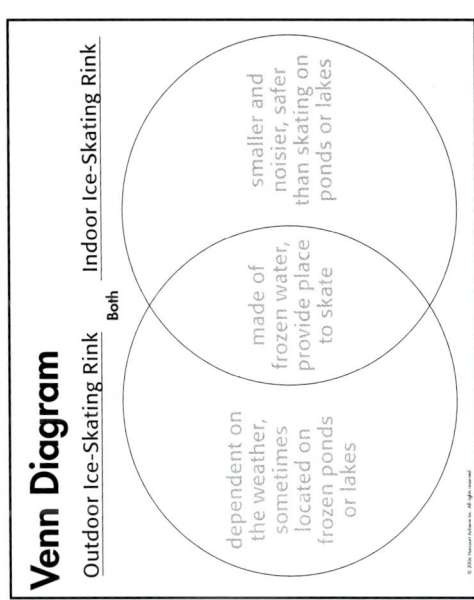

Directions: With children, fill in the Venn Diagram for *Ice-Skating*, comparing and contrasting indoor and outdoor rinks.

Discussion Questions

- What was this story about? (Literal)
- What kind of ice-skating rink would you use if you lived in a warm climate? Why? (Critical Thinking)
- At what kind of ice-skating rink do you think the narrator's parents prefer her to skate? (Inferential)

Activity Sheets

Word Wheel

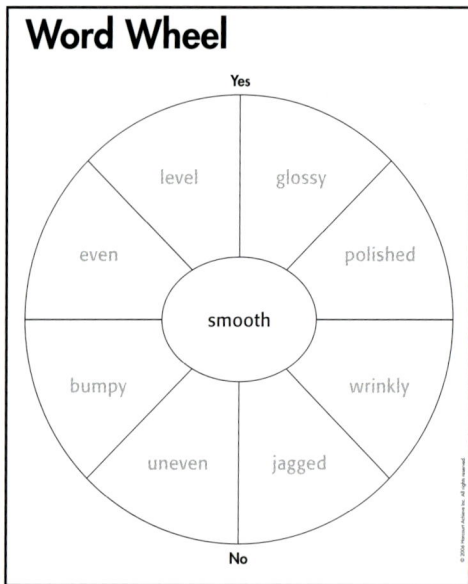

Directions: Have children fill in the Word Wheel using the word *smooth*.

Nonfiction Questions and Answers

Before Reading		During Reading	After Reading
What do I know about this topic?	What do I want to find out by reading this book?	What did I learn?	What new questions do I have?
It's harder to ice-skate than to roller-skate.	Are there any tricks I can learn?	There are two kinds of ice-skating rinks.	Where shouldn't you skate?
You can skate on a frozen pond.	How do you tell if the ice is thick enough?	It's safer to skate indoors.	Who checks the ice outside?

Directions: Have children fill in the Nonfiction Questions and Answers Chart about ice-skating rinks.

Optional: Ask children to write a journal entry based on the information in the chart.